STAR TREK™
CATS

BY JENNY PARKS

CHRONICLE BOOKS

SAN FRANCISCO

LIBRARY OF CONGRESS CATALOGING-IN-PUBLICATION DATA IS AVAILABLE.

ISBN: 978-1-4521-5841-9

MANUFACTURED IN CHINA

FSC
www.fsc.org

MIX
Paper from
responsible sources
FSC™ C020056

DESIGNED BY MICHAEL MORRIS

10 9 8 7 6 5 4 3 2 1

CHRONICLE BOOKS LLC
680 SECOND STREET
SAN FRANCISCO, CA 94107
WWW.CHRONICLEBOOKS.COM

To Mom and Dad, for the love of cats and sci-fi.

The Crew of the
U.S.S. Enterprise (NCC-1701)

Science Officer and
First Officer Spock

Captain James T. Kirk

Lt. Commander
Dr. Leonard "Bones" McCoy

Chief Engineer
Montgomery "Scotty" Scott

Lieutenant Nyota Uhura

Lieutenant Hikaru Sulu

Ensign Pavel Chekov

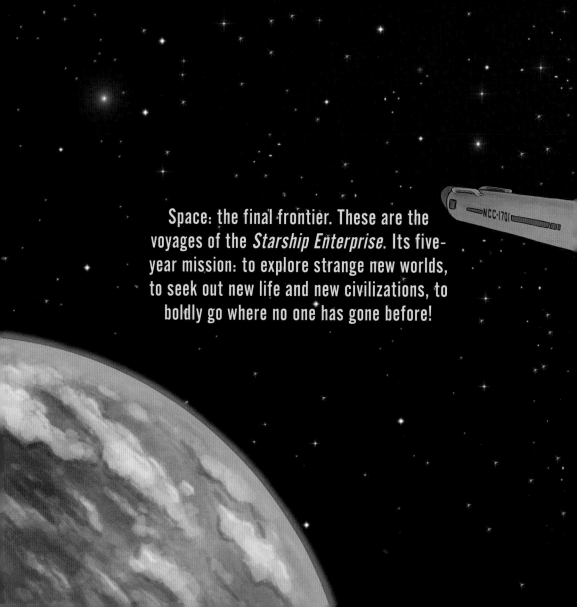

Space: the final frontier. These are the voyages of the *Starship Enterprise*. Its five-year mission: to explore strange new worlds, to seek out new life and new civilizations, to boldly go where no one has gone before!

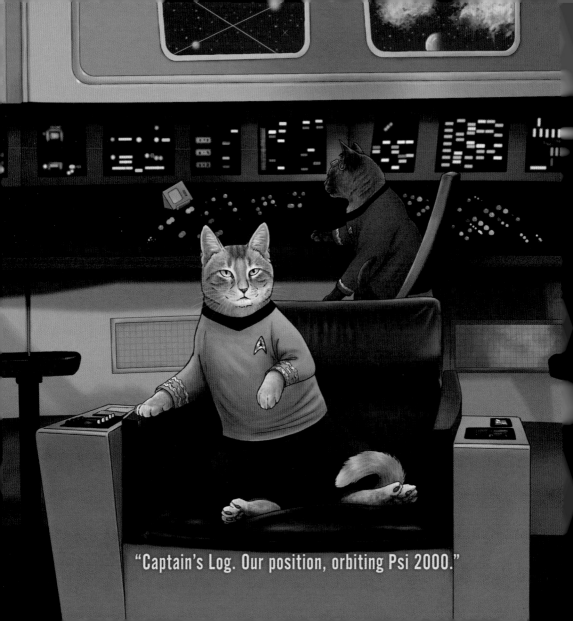

"Captain's Log. Our position, orbiting Psi 2000."

"An ancient world, now a frozen wasteland about to rip apart, in its death throes."

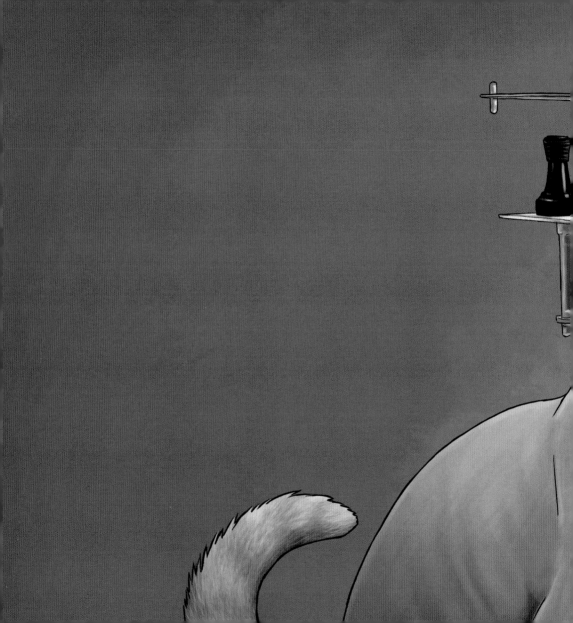

"Your illogical approach to chess does have its advantages on occasion, Captain."

"Cats in space, be wary, be wary!
We know not what he'll do."

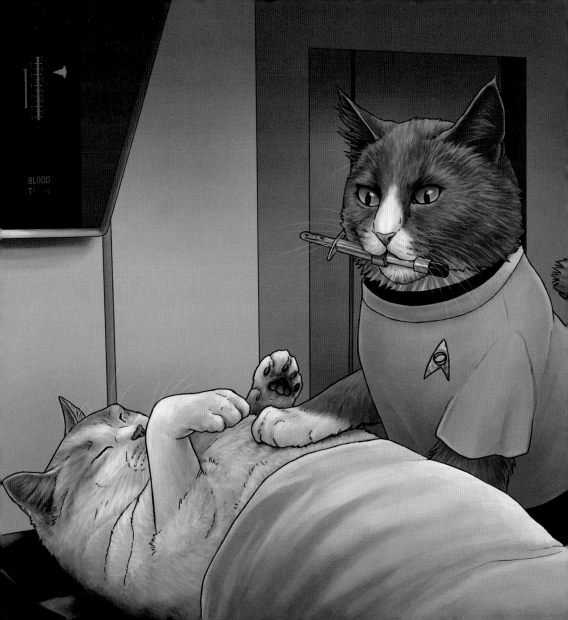

RESPIRATION

PULSE

ADJUST
FOR NORMAL

RECORDER
ON ⬭

| TEMP | BRAIN | LUNGS | | CELL |
| F   C | K3 | | | RATE |

"I'm not a magician, Spock, just an
old country doctor."

"Energize!"

"We compete for everything: power, fame, women—everything we desire, and it is our nature . . . to win."

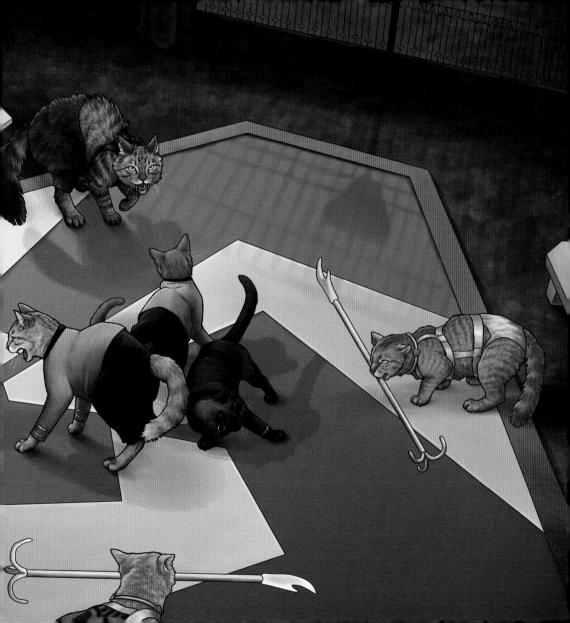

"Blast it! Do something! He's dying!"

"This combat . . ."

". . . is to the death."

"He's dead, Jim."

"Scotty, beam us up!"

"Red alert!"

"My mind to your mind,
my thoughts to your thoughts."

"Fear not, fair lady!"

"I cannae change the laws of physics!"

"Captain, although your abilities intrigue me,
you are quite honestly inferior."

"Laddie, don't you think you should . . . rephrase that?"

"Live long and prosper."

JENNY PARKS is a nerd and freelance illustrator with a degree in scientific illustration, and a love for drawing animals. For the last several years she has been specializing in painting cats dressed as pop-culture characters, splitting her time between freelance work and tabling at comic book conventions around the country. She currently resides in Denver, Colorado with her two cats, Mab and Mamoko, fulfilling her destiny to make a living drawing cute, fuzzy things. www.jennyparks.com

This book wouldn't have been possible without the help and support of so many awesome people. Thanks to my brother, Gregory for encouraging me to sell my work at my first San Diego Comic-Con, and a million hugs and thanks to Becca Charlton, Dailen Ogden, and Faith Williams——you know what you did. Thanks to Lee Akamichi, without whom I might not have majored in art, and special thanks to Wynn Rankin, Michael Morris, Lia Brown, Beth Steiner, Pippa White, Sandy Smith, April Whitney, and everyone at Chronicle Books for even giving me the chance to make this book a reality. Lastly: thanks to cats for existing.

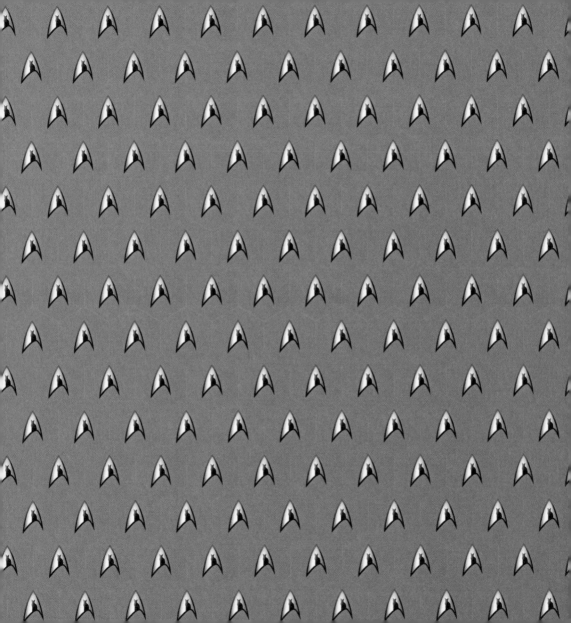